Preschool Tracing

Volume 1

ALPHABET-CAPITAL LETTERS

NAME

DATE

DIRECTIONS: PRACTICE WRITING EACH LETTER IN THE SPACE PROVIDED.

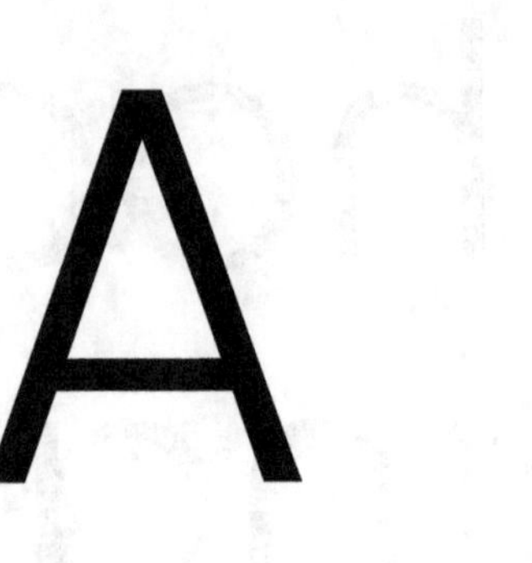

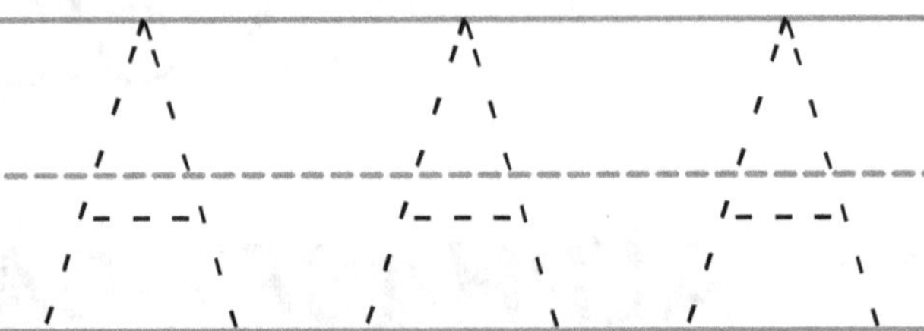

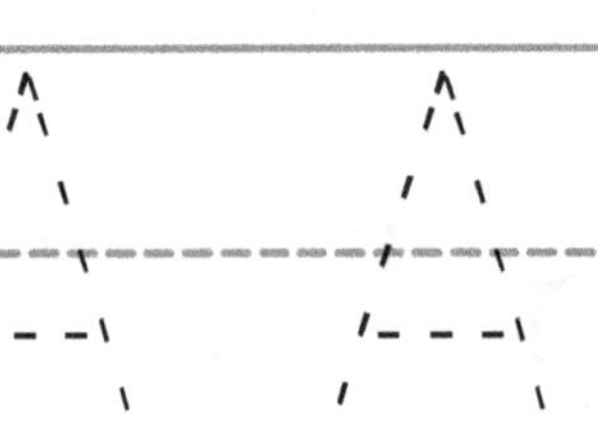

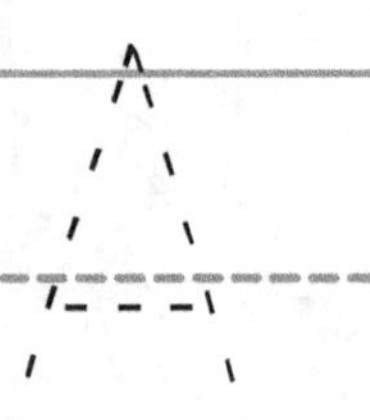

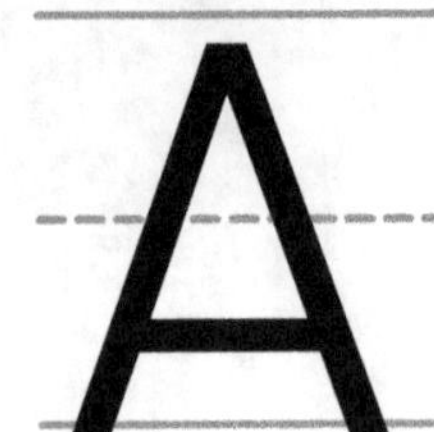

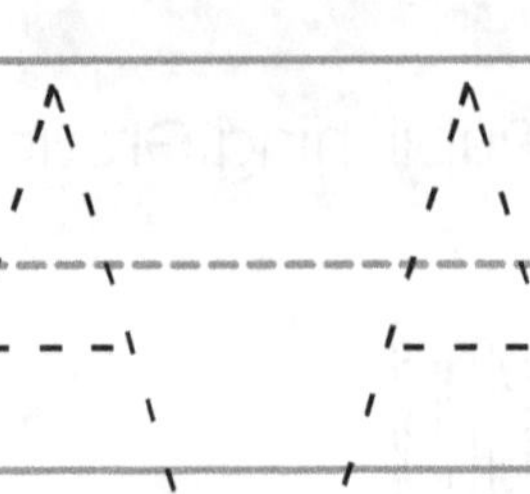

Name:

DIRECTIONS: COPY THE CAPITAL LETTER

A

A

A

A

A

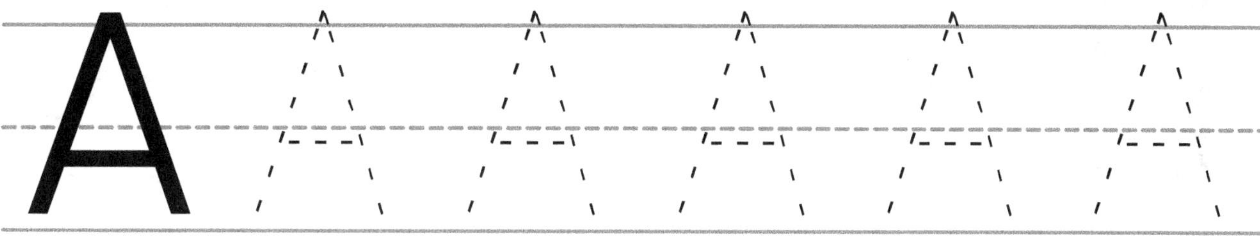

NAME

DATE

DIRECTIONS: PRACTICE WRITING EACH LETTER IN THE SPACE PROVIDED.

B

B

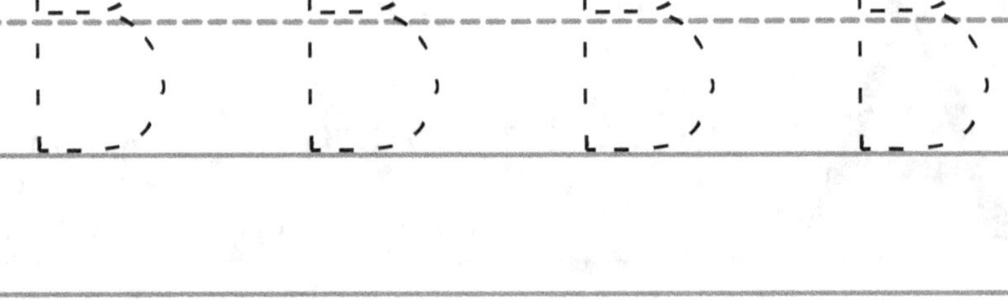

B

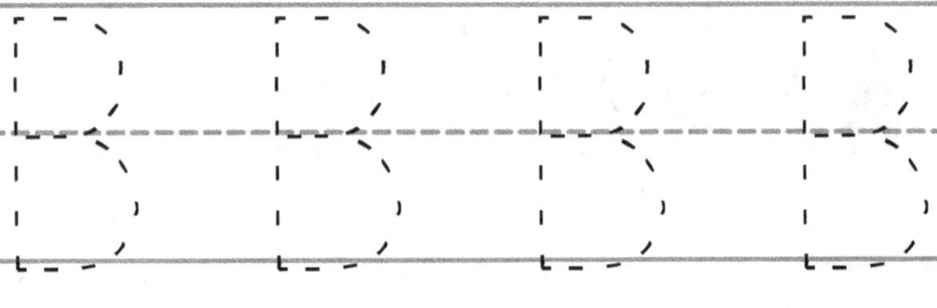

B

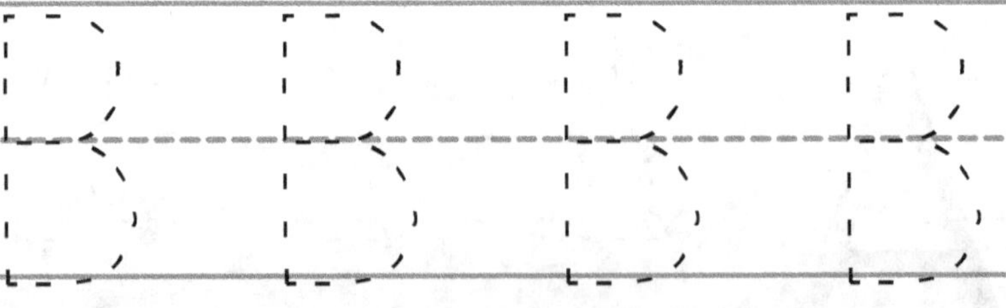

B

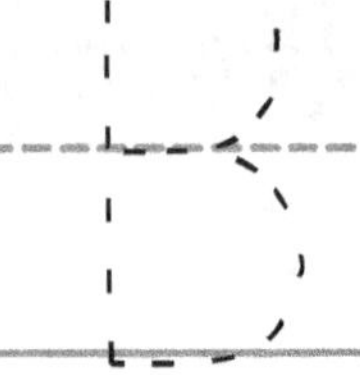

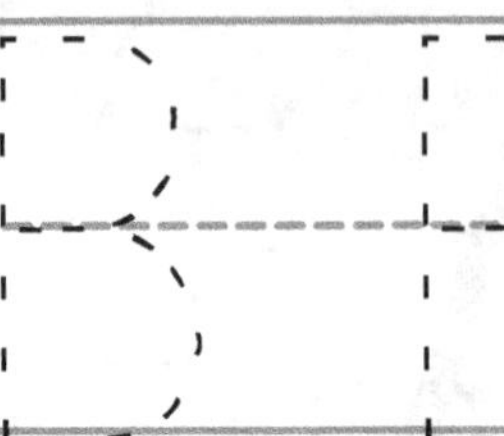

Name: ______________________________

DIRECTIONS: COPY THE CAPITAL LETTER

B B B B B B

B B B B B B

B B B B B B

B B B B B B

B B B B B B

B B B B B B

NAME

DATE

DIRECTIONS: PRACTICE WRITING EACH LETTER IN THE SPACE PROVIDED.

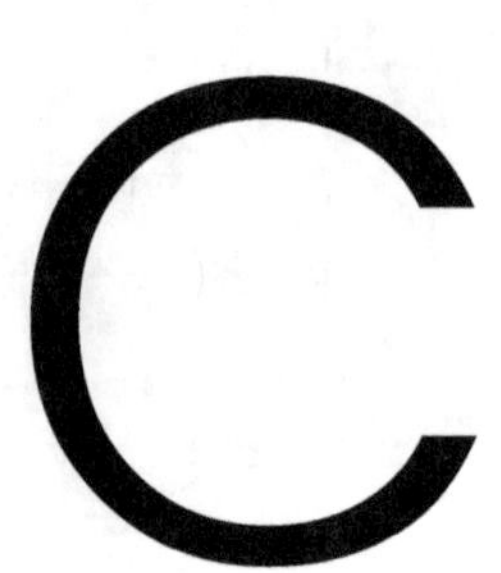

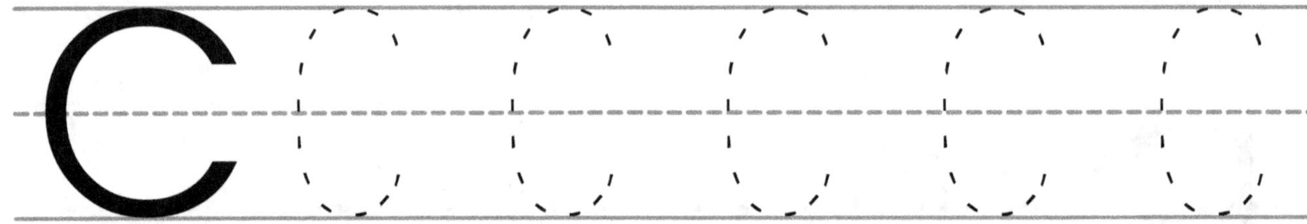

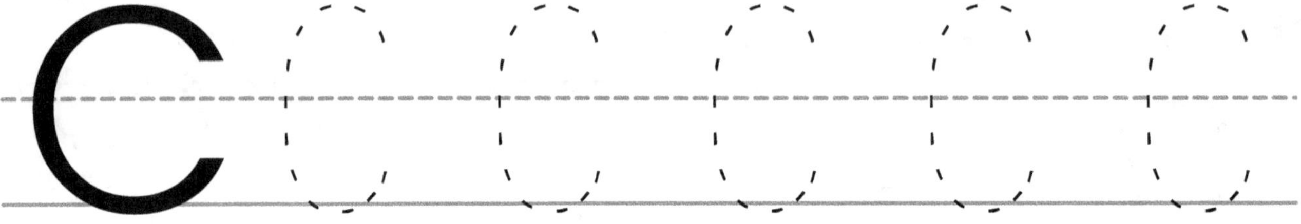

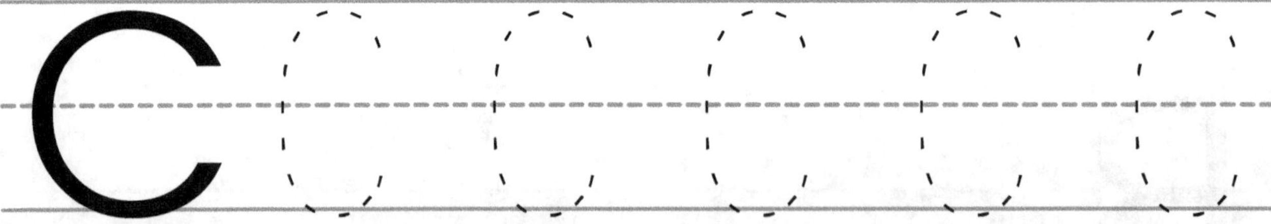

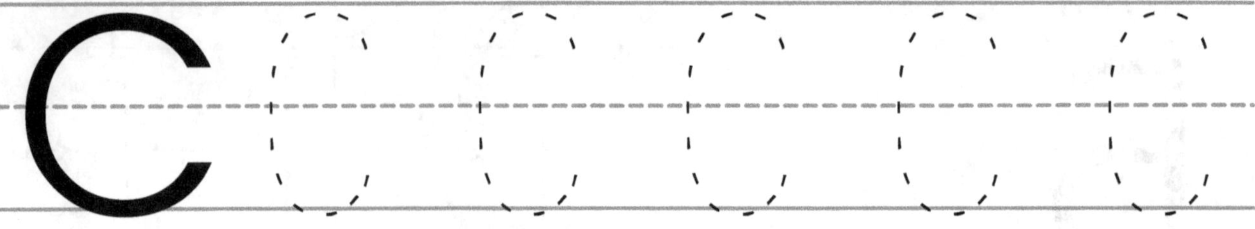

Name:

DIRECTIONS: COPY THE CAPITAL LETTER

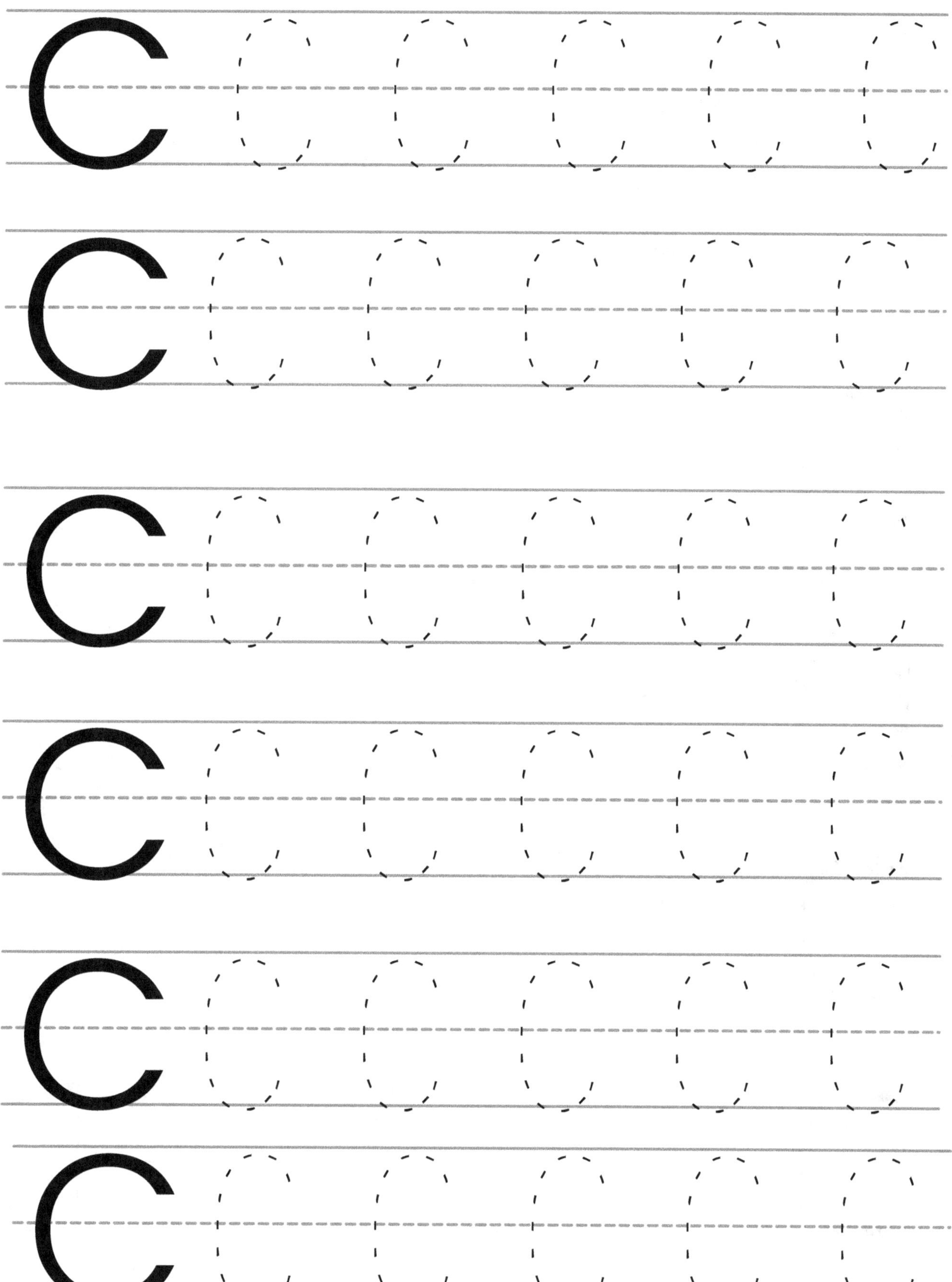

NAME

DATE

DIRECTIONS: PRACTICE WRITING EACH LETTER IN THE SPACE PROVIDED.

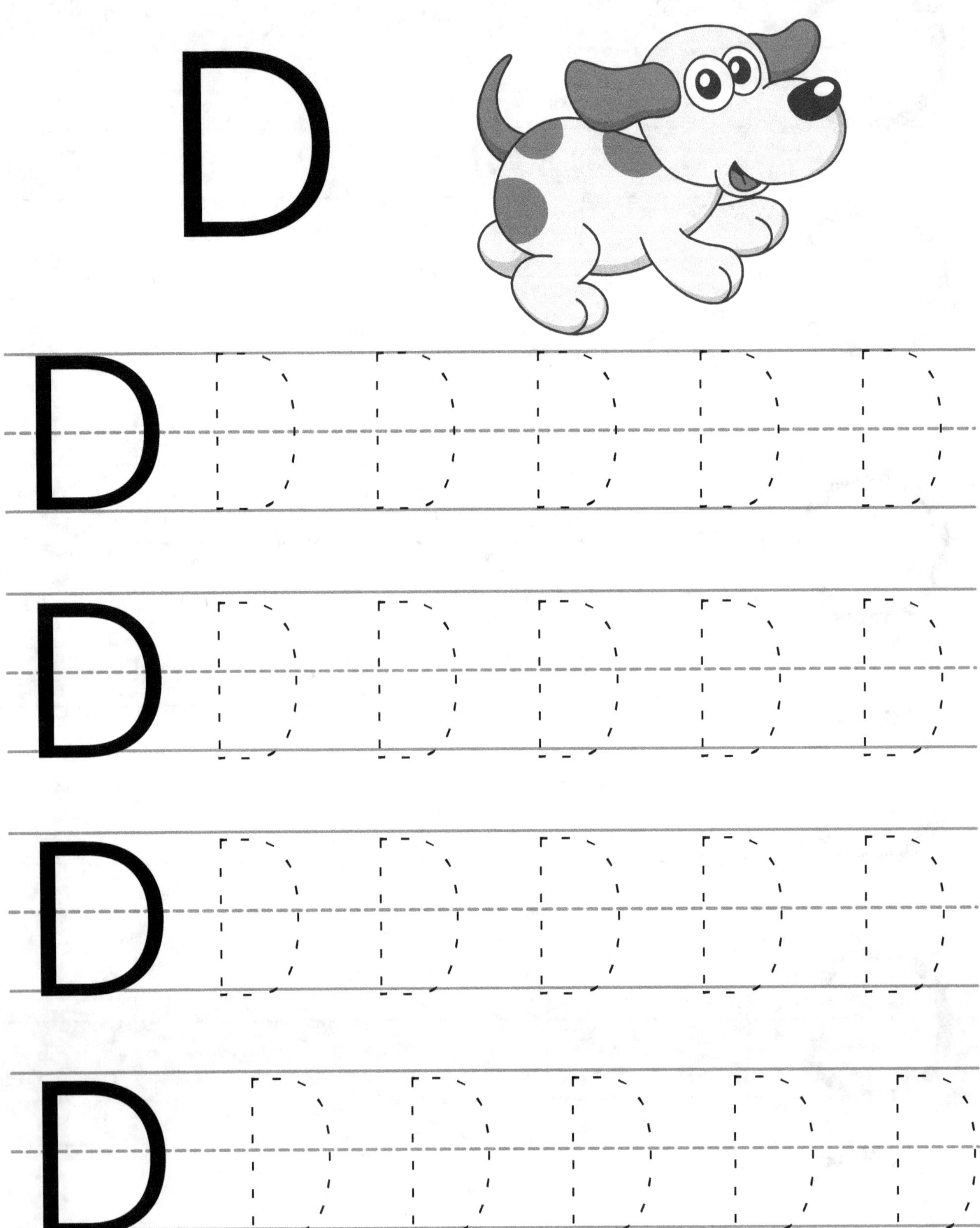

Name:

DIRECTIONS: COPY THE CAPITAL LETTER

D

D

D

D

D

D

NAME

DATE

DIRECTIONS: PRACTICE WRITING EACH LETTER IN THE SPACE PROVIDED.

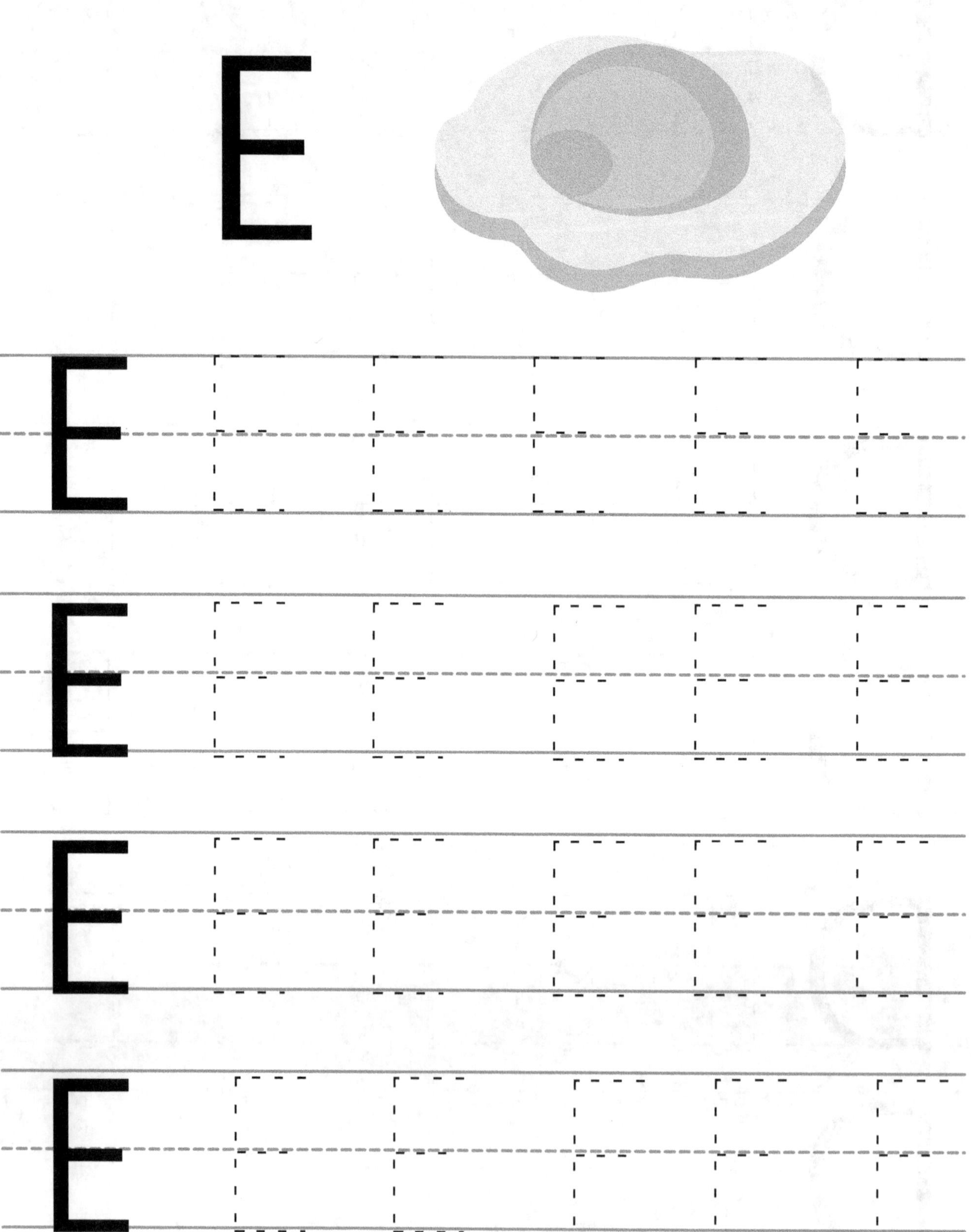

Name:

DIRECTIONS: COPY THE CAPITAL LETTER

E

E

E

E

E

E

NAME

DATE

DIRECTIONS: PRACTICE WRITING EACH LETTER IN THE SPACE PROVIDED.

Name: ____________________

DIRECTIONS: COPY THE CAPITAL LETTER

F

F

F

F

F

F

NAME

DATE

DIRECTIONS: PRACTICE WRITING EACH LETTER IN THE SPACE PROVIDED.

Name: ______________________

DIRECTIONS: COPY THE CAPITAL LETTER

NAME

DATE

DIRECTIONS: PRACTICE WRITING EACH LETTER IN THE SPACE PROVIDED.

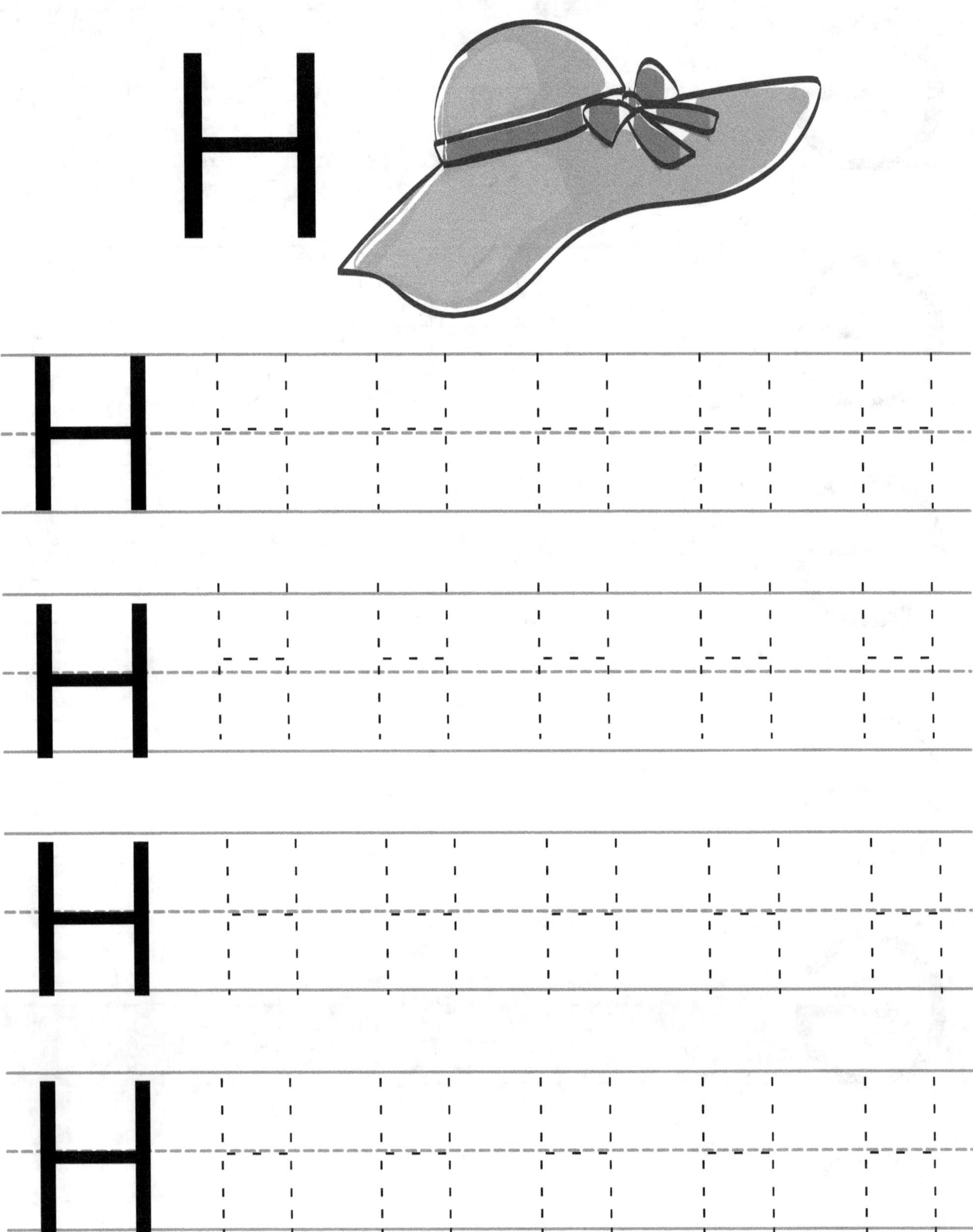

Name:

DIRECTIONS: COPY THE CAPITAL LETTER

H

H

H

H

H

H

NAME

DATE

DIRECTIONS: PRACTICE WRITING EACH LETTER IN THE SPACE PROVIDED.

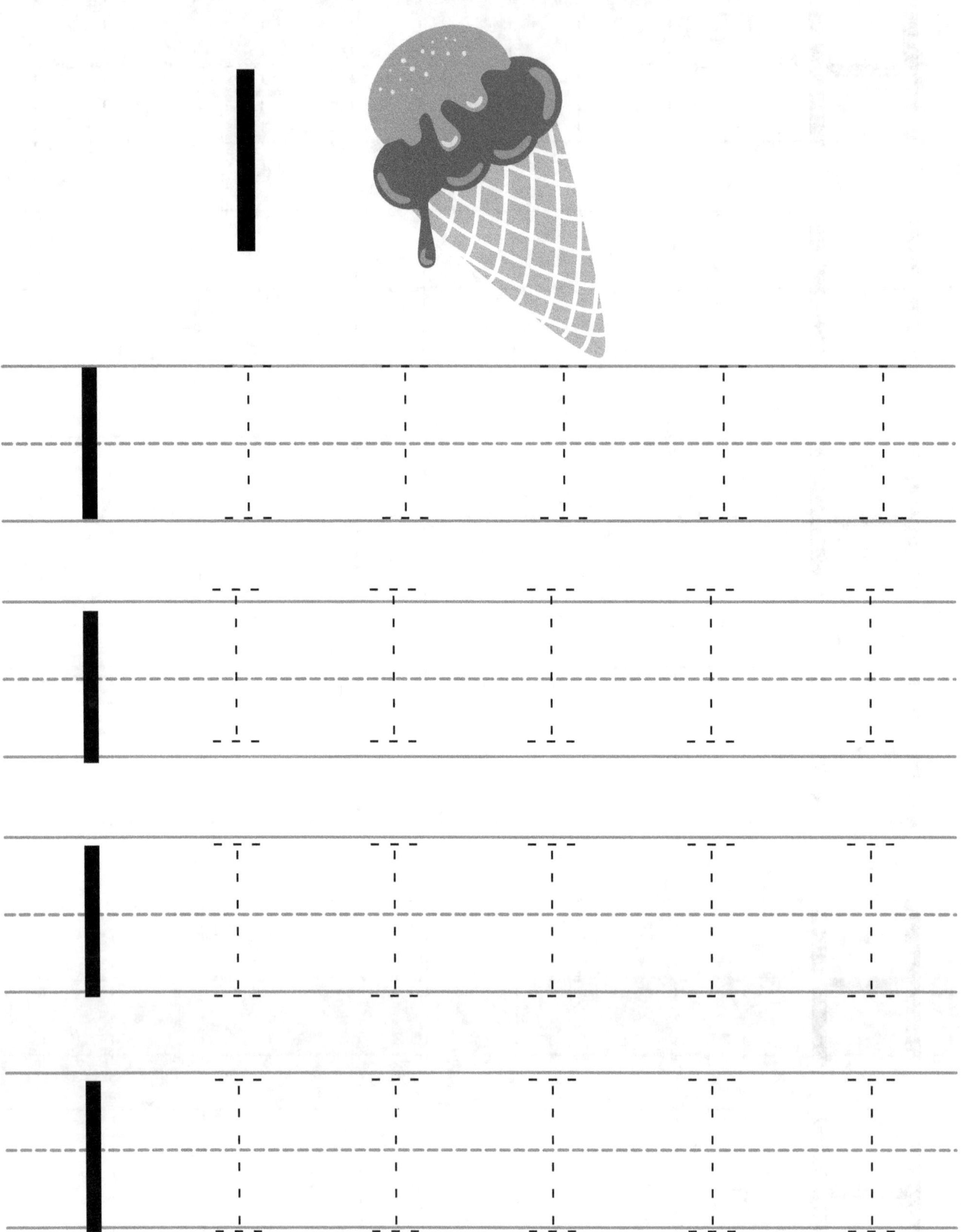

Name: ______________________

DIRECTIONS: COPY THE CAPITAL LETTER

NAME

DATE

DIRECTIONS: PRACTICE WRITING EACH LETTER IN THE SPACE PROVIDED.

Name: ______________________________

DIRECTIONS: COPY THE CAPITAL LETTER

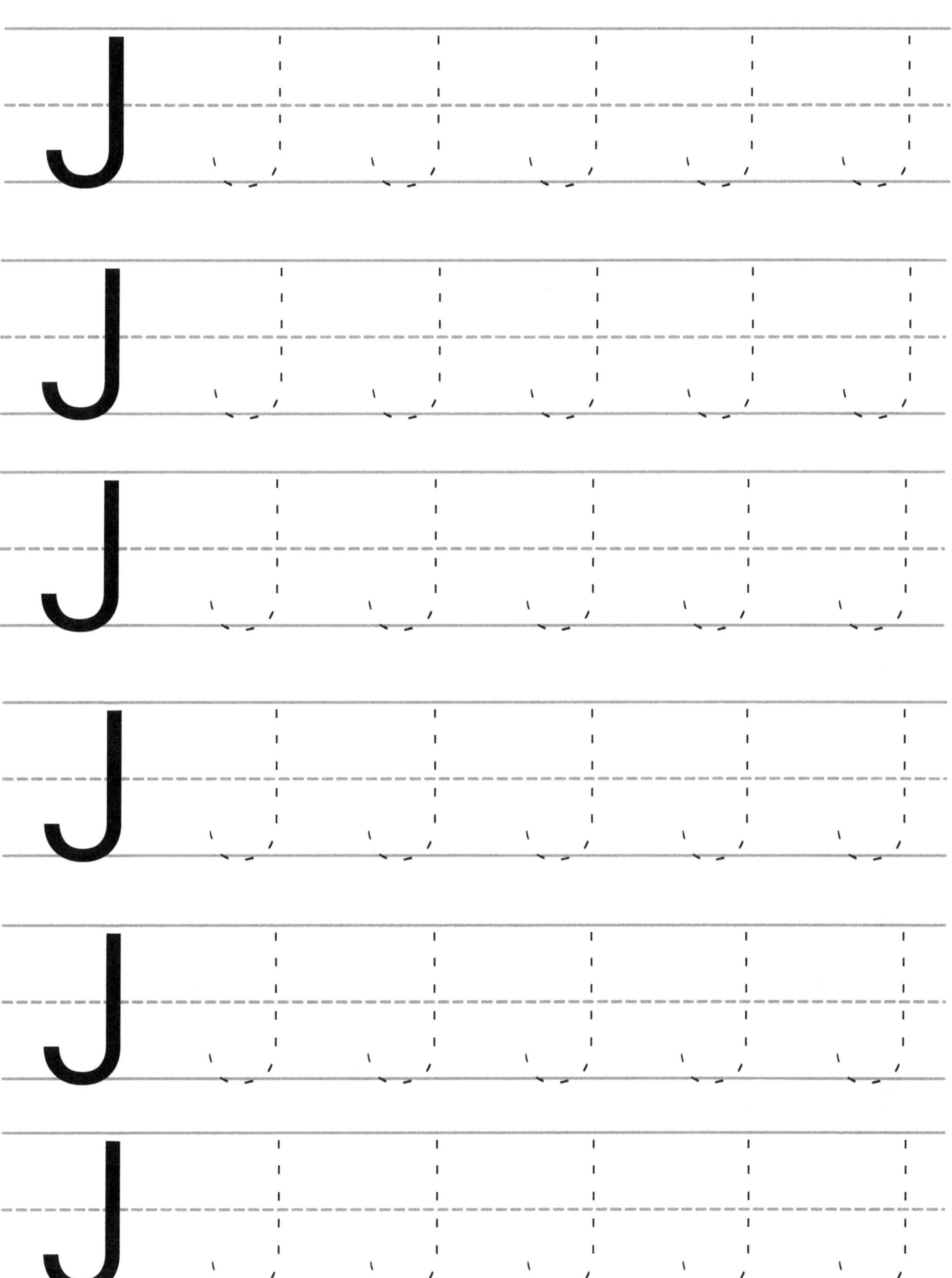

NAME

DATE

DIRECTIONS: PRACTICE WRITING EACH LETTER IN THE SPACE PROVIDED.

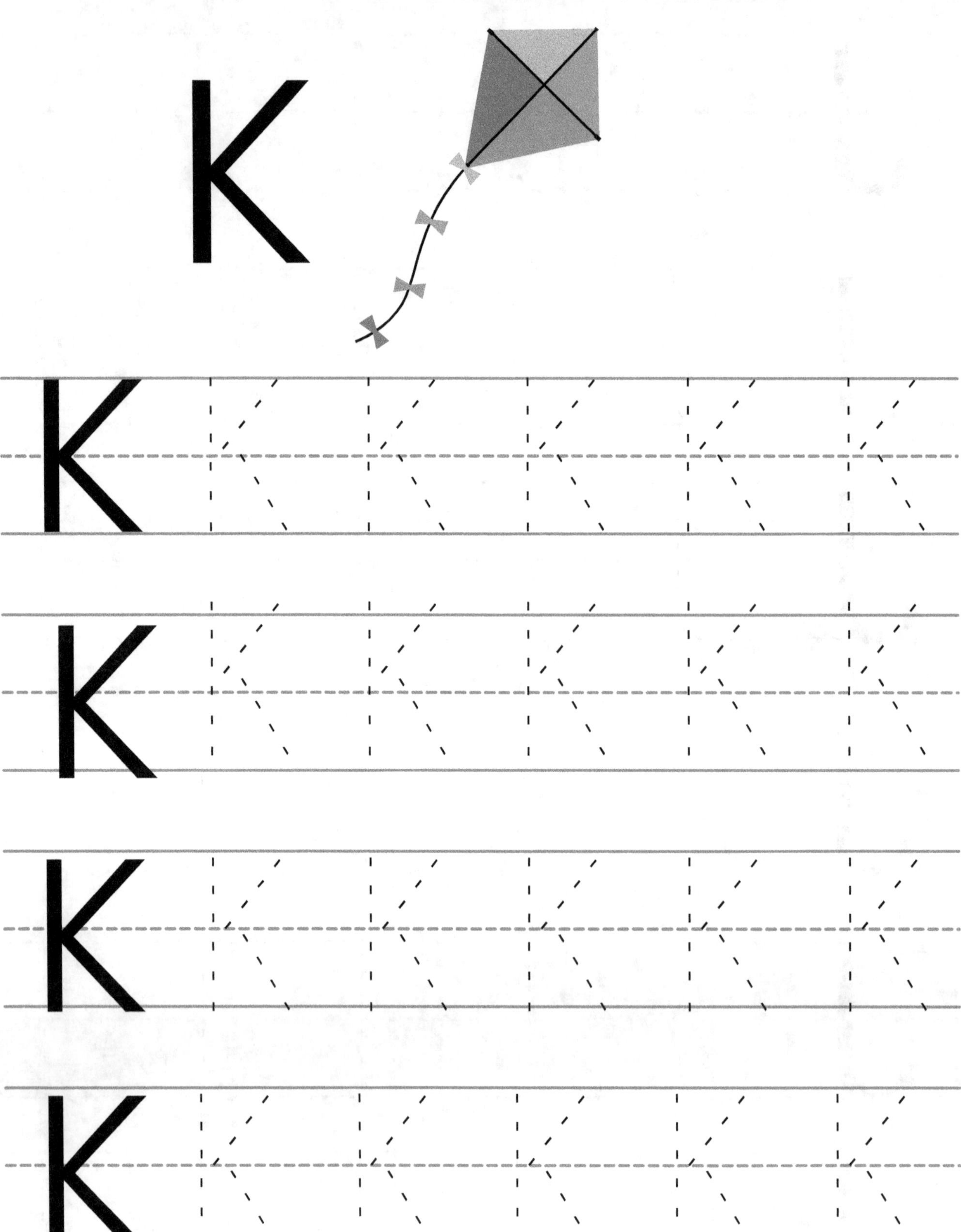

Name:

DIRECTIONS: COPY THE CAPITAL LETTER

K

K

K

K

K

K

NAME

DATE

DIRECTIONS: PRACTICE WRITING EACH LETTER IN THE SPACE PROVIDED.

Name:

DIRECTIONS: COPY THE CAPITAL LETTER

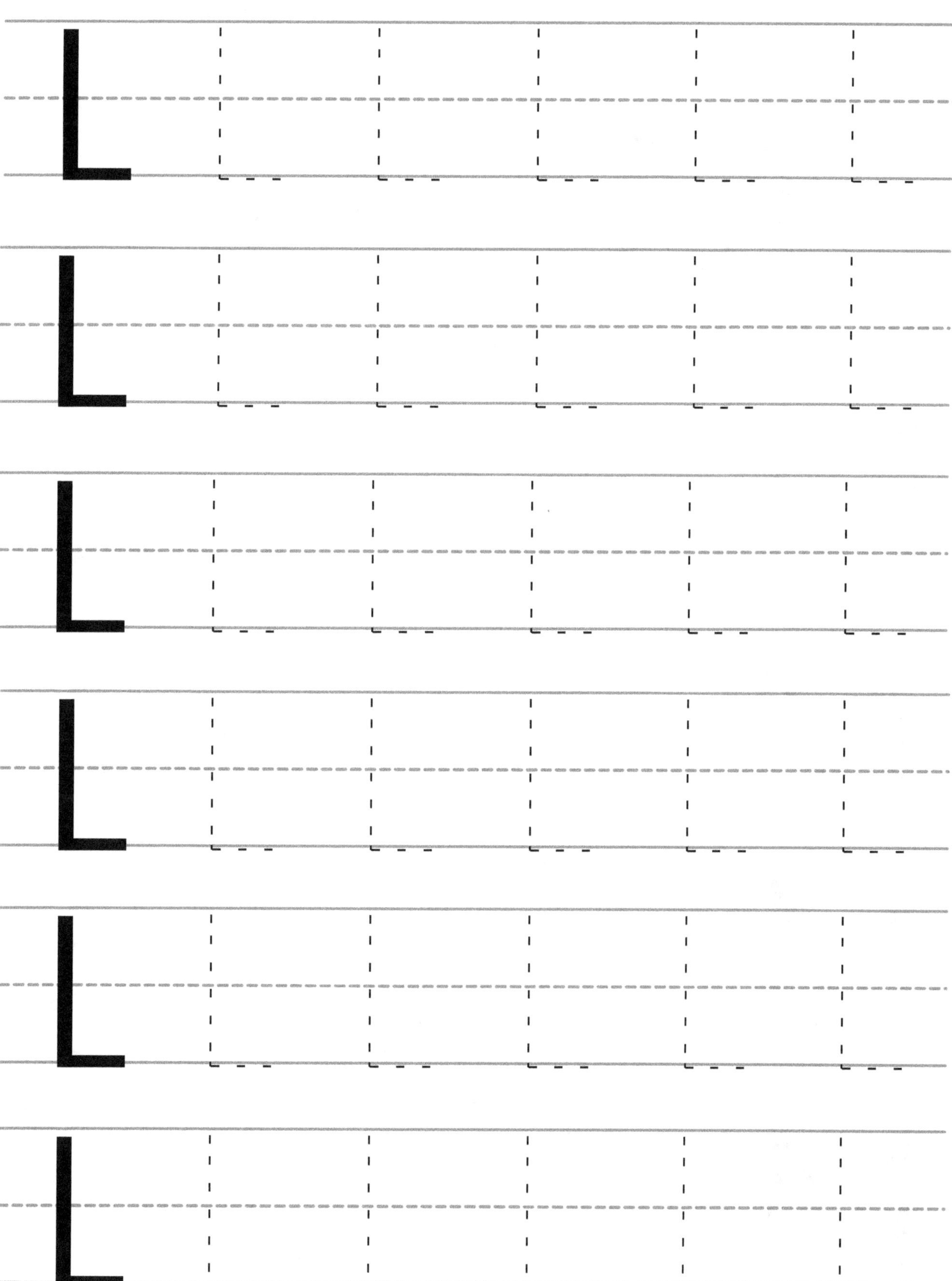

NAME

DATE

DIRECTIONS: PRACTICE WRITING EACH LETTER IN THE SPACE PROVIDED.

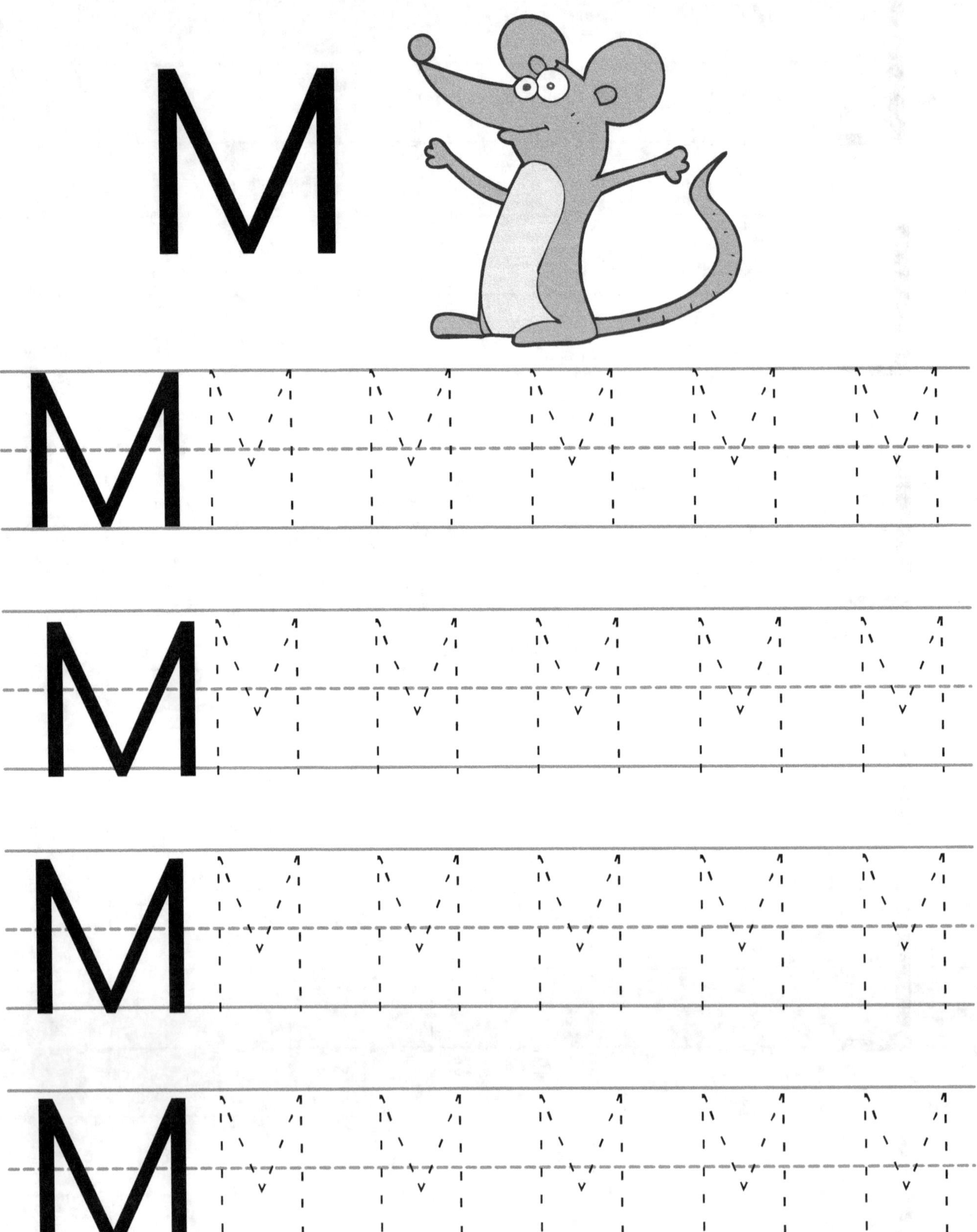

Name:

DIRECTIONS: COPY THE CAPITAL LETTER

M

M

M

M

M

M

NAME

DATE

DIRECTIONS: PRACTICE WRITING EACH LETTER IN THE SPACE PROVIDED.

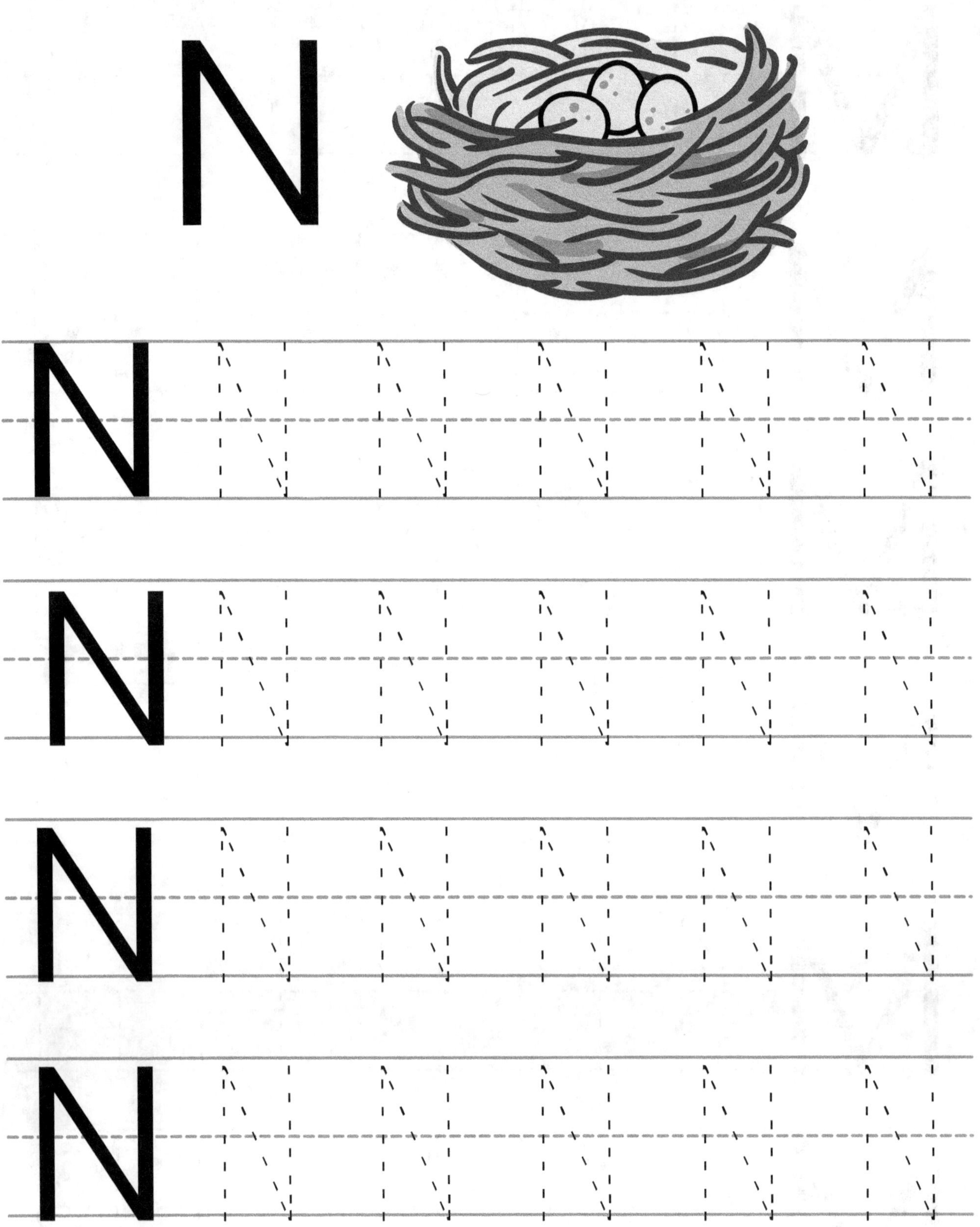

Name:

DIRECTIONS: COPY THE CAPITAL LETTER

N

N

N

N

N

N

NAME

DATE

DIRECTIONS: PRACTICE WRITING EACH LETTER IN THE SPACE PROVIDED.

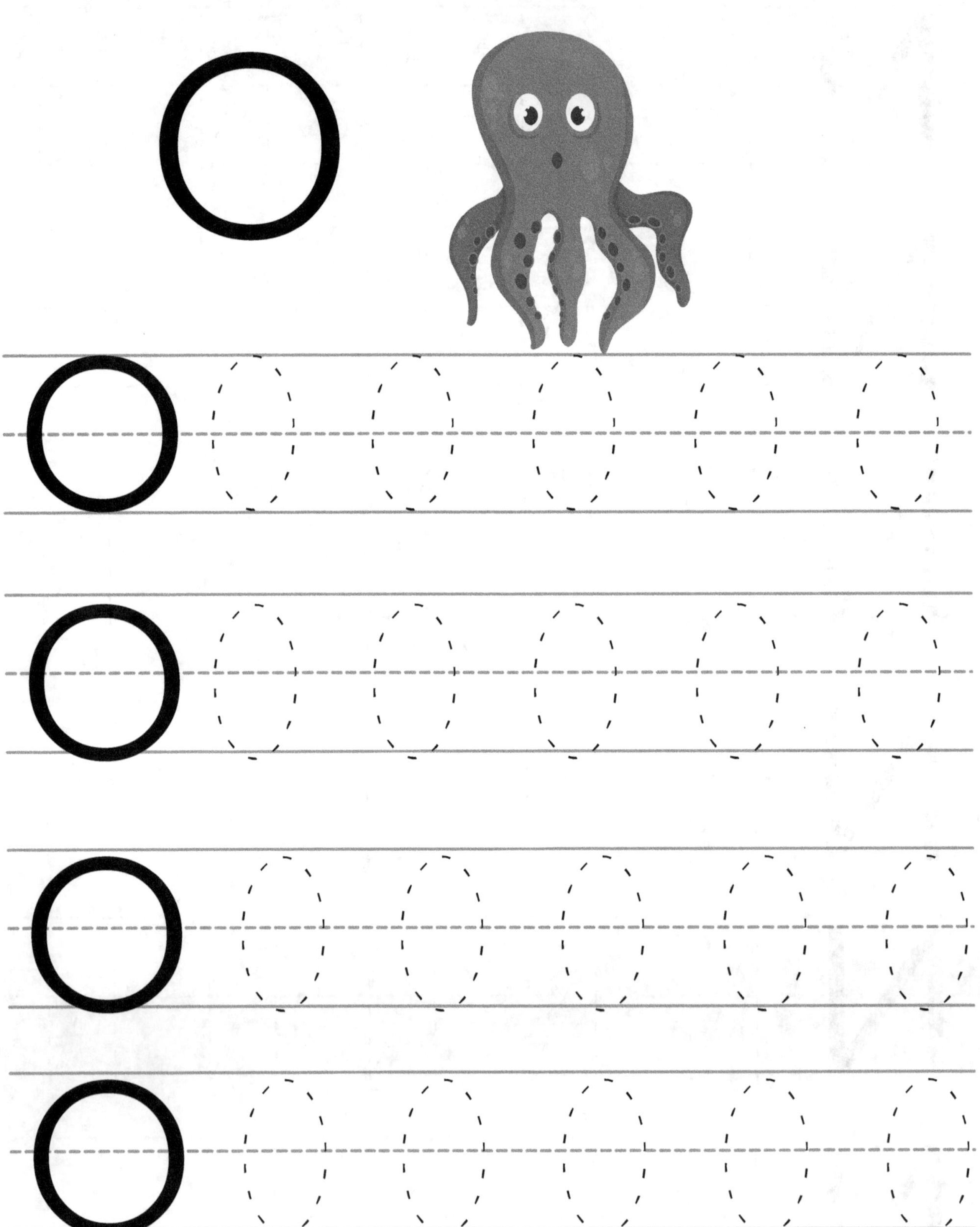

Name:

DIRECTIONS: COPY THE CAPITAL LETTER

O

O

O

O

O

O

NAME

DATE

DIRECTIONS: PRACTICE WRITING EACH LETTER IN THE SPACE PROVIDED.

P

P

P

P

P

Name:

DIRECTIONS: COPY THE CAPITAL LETTER

P

P

P

P

P

P

NAME

DATE

DIRECTIONS: PRACTICE WRITING EACH LETTER IN THE SPACE PROVIDED.

Name:

DIRECTIONS: COPY THE CAPITAL LETTER

Q

Q

Q

Q

Q

Q

NAME

DATE

DIRECTIONS: PRACTICE WRITING EACH LETTER IN THE SPACE PROVIDED.

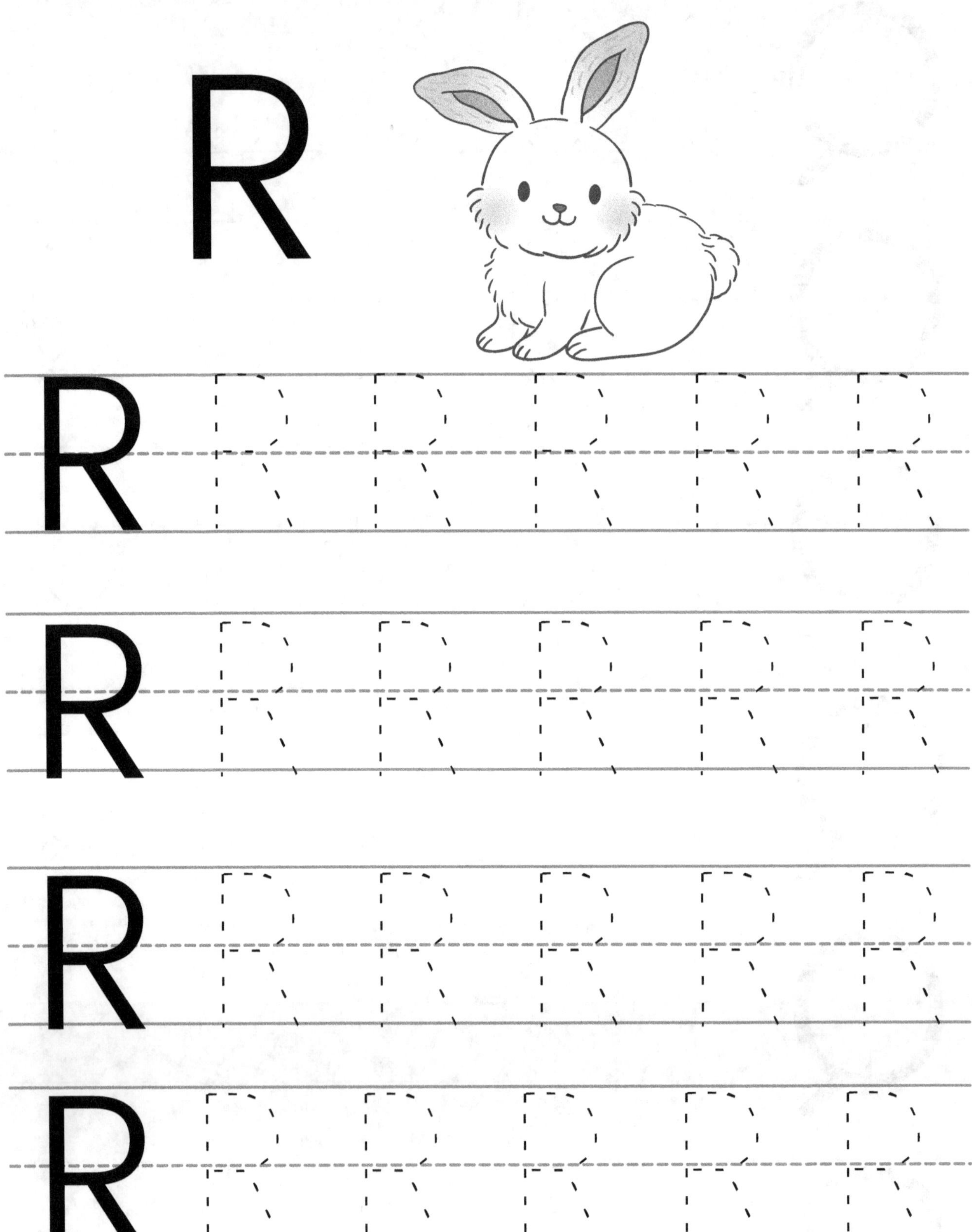

Name:

DIRECTIONS: COPY THE CAPITAL LETTER

R

R

R

R

R

R

NAME

DATE

DIRECTIONS: PRACTICE WRITING EACH LETTER IN THE SPACE PROVIDED.

Name:

DIRECTIONS: COPY THE CAPITAL LETTER

S

S

S

S

S

S

NAME

DATE

DIRECTIONS: PRACTICE WRITING EACH LETTER IN THE SPACE PROVIDED.

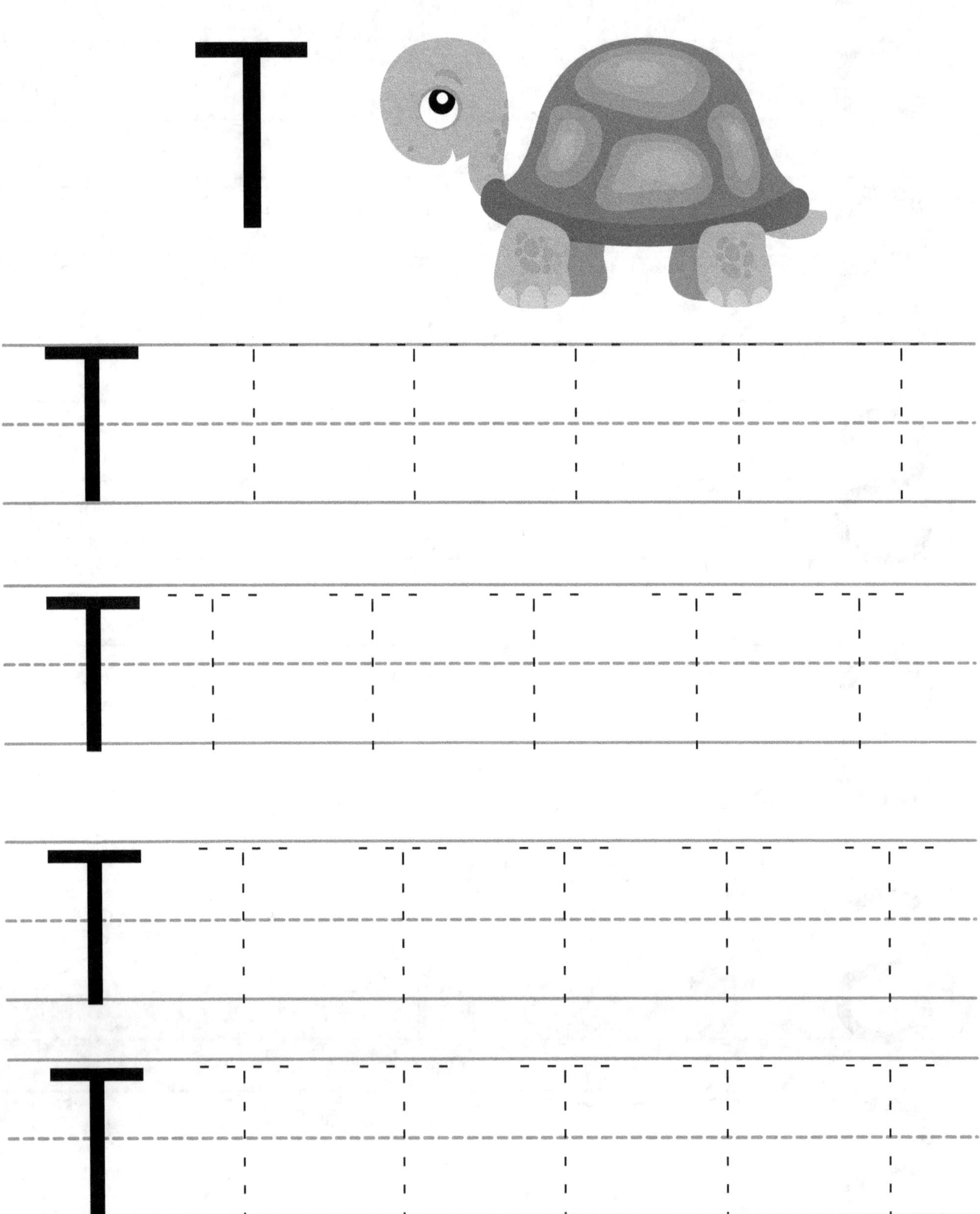

Name:

DIRECTIONS: COPY THE CAPITAL LETTER

T

T

T

T

T

T

NAME

DATE

DIRECTIONS: PRACTICE WRITING EACH LETTER IN THE SPACE PROVIDED.

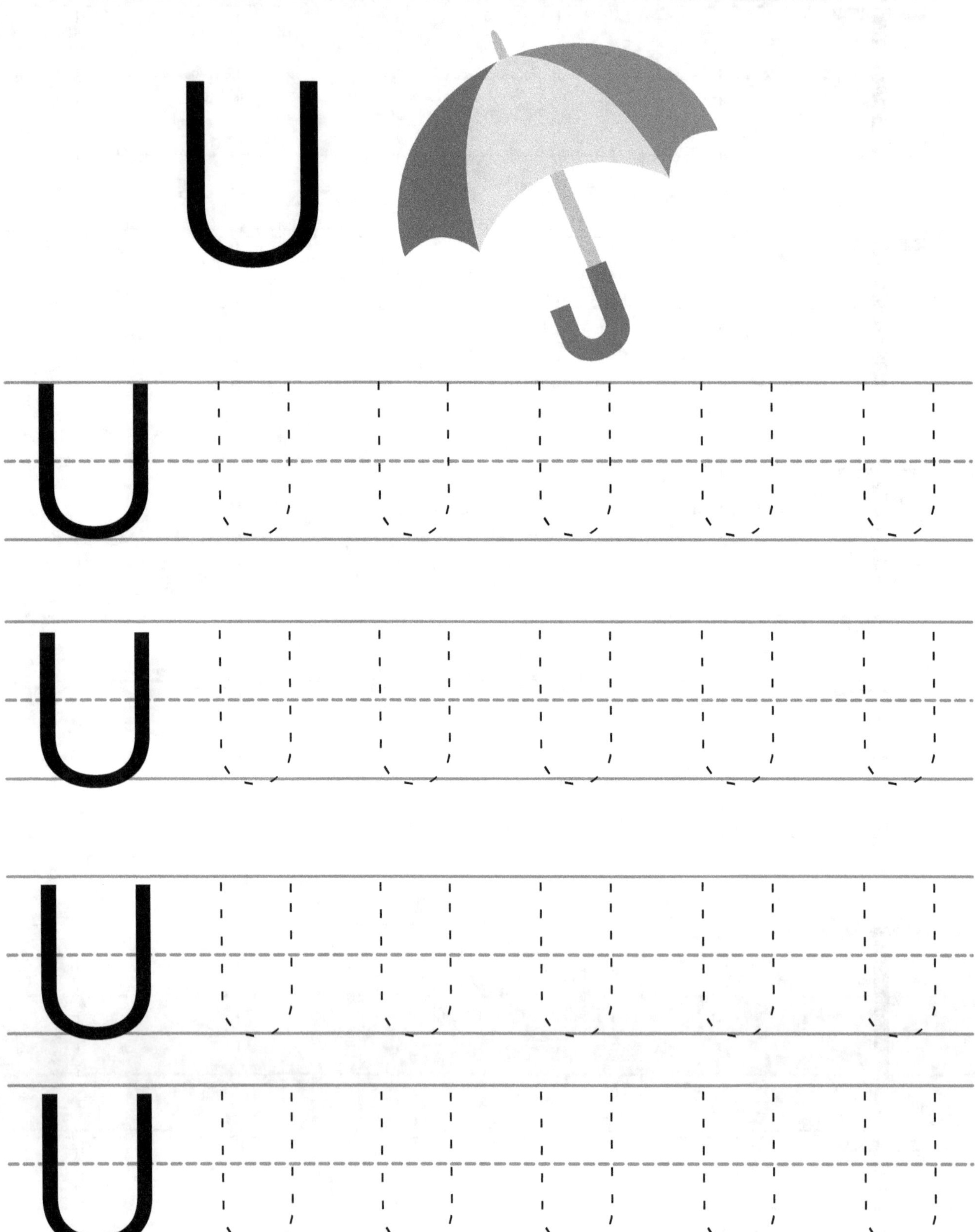

Name: ______________________

DIRECTIONS: COPY THE CAPITAL LETTER

U

U

U

U

U

U

NAME

DATE

DIRECTIONS: PRACTICE WRITING EACH LETTER IN THE SPACE PROVIDED.

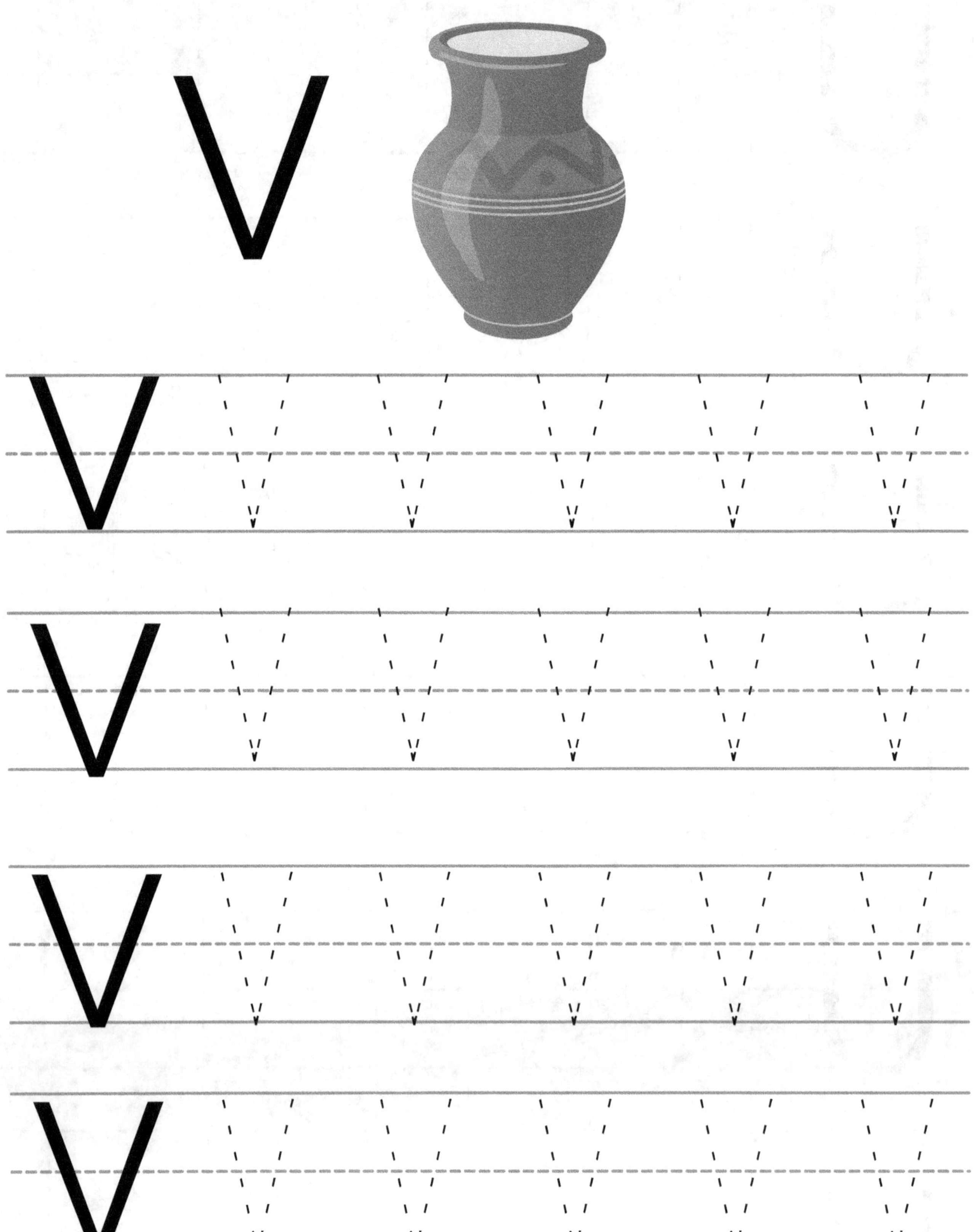

Name:

DIRECTIONS: COPY THE CAPITAL LETTER

V

V

V

V

V

V

NAME

DATE

DIRECTIONS: PRACTICE WRITING EACH LETTER IN THE SPACE PROVIDED.

W

W

W

W

W

Name: ______________________

DIRECTIONS: COPY THE CAPITAL LETTER

W

W

W

W

W

W

NAME

DATE

DIRECTIONS: PRACTICE WRITING EACH LETTER IN THE SPACE PROVIDED.

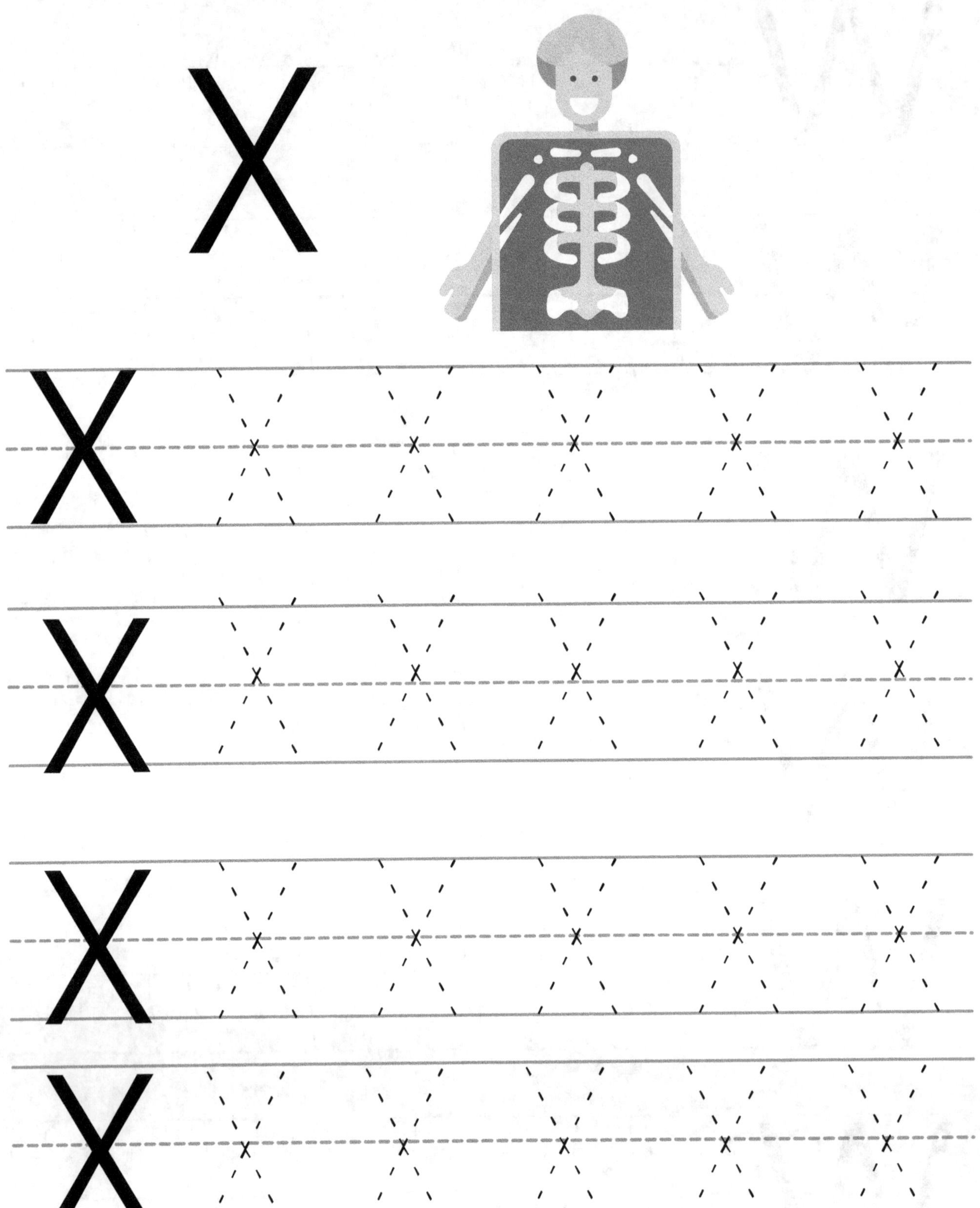

Name:

DIRECTIONS: COPY THE CAPITAL LETTER

X X X X X X

X X X X X X

X X X X X X

X X X X X X

X X X X X X

X X X X X X

NAME

DATE

DIRECTIONS: PRACTICE WRITING EACH LETTER IN THE SPACE PROVIDED.

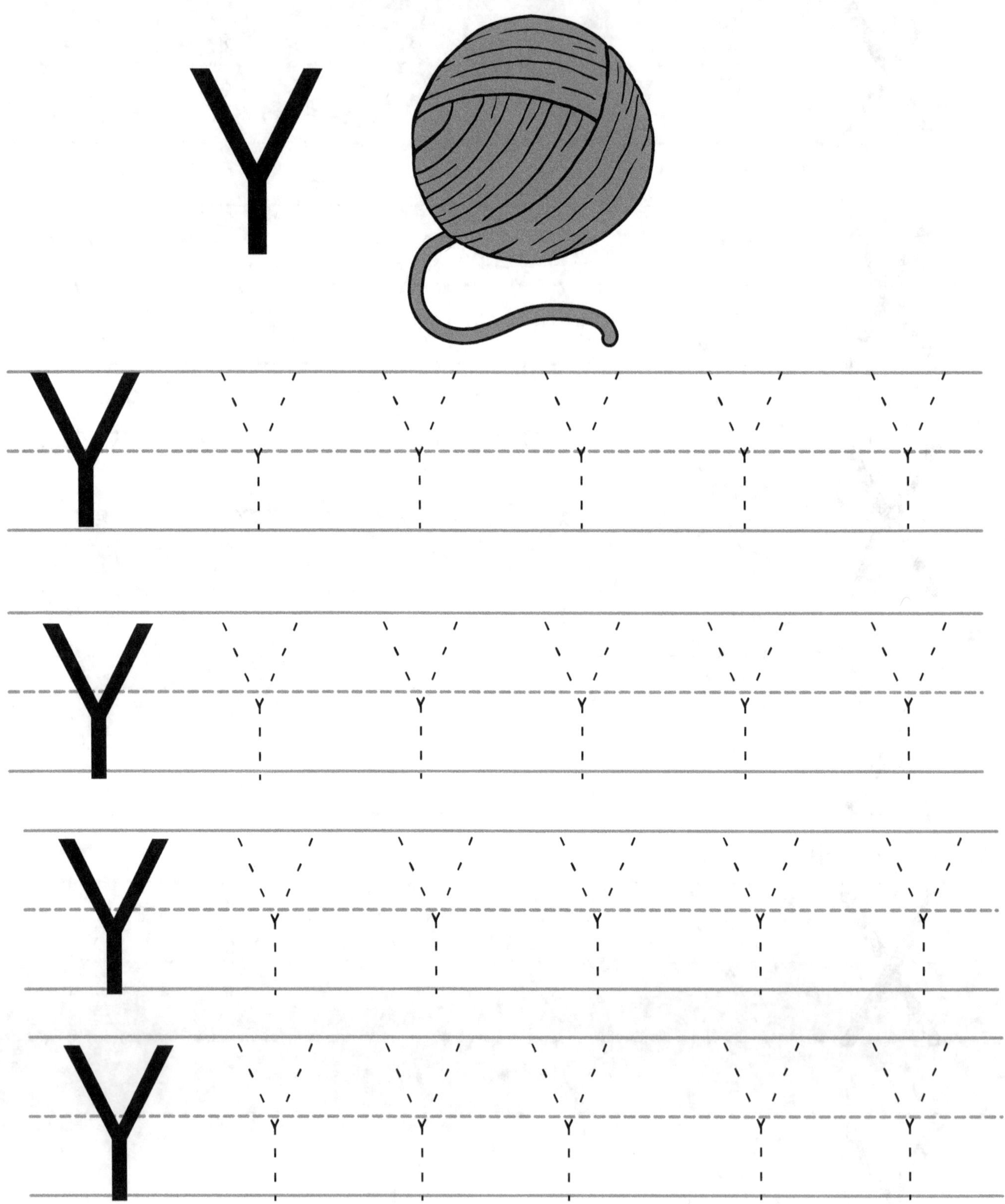

Name:

DIRECTIONS: COPY THE CAPITAL LETTER

Y Y Y Y Y Y

Y Y Y Y Y Y

Y Y Y Y Y Y

Y Y Y Y Y Y

Y Y Y Y Y Y

Y Y Y Y Y Y

NAME

DATE

DIRECTIONS: PRACTICE WRITING EACH LETTER IN THE SPACE PROVIDED.

Z

Z

Z

Z

Z

Name:

DIRECTIONS: COPY THE CAPITAL LETTER

Z

Z

Z

Z

Z

Z

Name:

FREE PRACTICE

Name:

FREE PRACTICE

Name:

FREE PRACTICE

Name:

FREE PRACTICE

Name:

FREE PRACTICE

Name:

FREE PRACTICE

Name:

FREE PRACTICE

Name:

FREE PRACTICE

Name:

FREE PRACTICE

Name:

FREE PRACTICE

Name:

FREE PRACTICE

Name:

FREE PRACTICE

Name:

FREE PRACTICE

Name:

FREE PRACTICE

Name:

FREE PRACTICE

Name:

FREE PRACTICE

Name:

FREE PRACTICE

Name:

FREE PRACTICE

Name:

FREE PRACTICE

Name:

FREE PRACTICE

Name:

FREE PRACTICE

Name:

FREE PRACTICE

Name:

FREE PRACTICE

Name:

FREE PRACTICE

Name:

FREE PRACTICE

Name:

FREE PRACTICE

www.ingramcontent.com/pod-product-compliance
Lightning Source LLC
LaVergne TN
LVHW080926110826
845155LV00039B/219

* 9 7 8 1 9 5 1 1 9 7 1 9 3 *